GUIDED

ACCOUNTABILITY

INCREASE THE LIKELIHOOD OF GOAL ACHIEVEMENT BY 97%

CHARLENA SMITH

Guided Accountability:
Increase the Likelihood of Goal Achievement by 97%

Copyright © 2019 by Charlena Smith

Cover Design by 100Covers.com
Interior Design by FormattedBooks.com

CONTENTS

ACKNOWLEDGMENTS

Be sure to read the last paragraph, because it's about you.

What an incredible joy it was to write *Guided Accountability*. The book, I mean. This acknowledgment part? It's really difficult for me. I've saved it for last and delayed printing because of it. Not because I don't have plenty of people to acknowledge – Oh, NO. It 100% takes a village to publish a book like this. It's so very difficult because there are SO. MANY. AMAZING humans out there who have helped to bring this book to life. So, so many. Honestly, I've saved this part for last – because it's the most difficult for me. But my *Guided Accountability* partner is holding me to my promise, so here we go...

Since the journey that brought us *Guided Accountability* as a concept evolved in stages, or parts, if you will, I'll address my acknowledgments in those same parts.

MY EVERYTHING

Scott. What words could I ever write that embody all that you mean to me? You gave me life the day we met. My heart was set on fire like I didn't believe was possible. You blessed me with our two greatest gifts: Keegan and Colby. You held my hand through all of the pain and heartache. You bore the weight of the world on your shoulders. And you saved my life. But you know that. You pored over medical journals, outlined experimental practices to try, and stayed in lockstep with every "round" of doctors who came through. You made them believe I could make it. You made them see the impossible as possible. You created a new reality for them to step into – a reality that included a happy, healthy me at the end. You held my hand through therapy after intense therapy. You supported me in my year of "Be," when I refused to put anything but you and the boys back in my jar. You supported me in my nonprofit. You supported me through the birth of Optio. And you supported me in the writing of this book. You show up, as your best self, EVERY day. Every single day. You will always be my hero. Without you – this is all meaningless. Thank you. Thank you for making my world complete.

Keegan and Colby, what champions you have been. You fought hard to come into this world. You fought hard every day in the womb, and you fought your whole first year to catch up. You've witnessed trauma. True trauma. And you came out the other side better for it. The way you support one another is unlike anything I've ever experienced. I am so, so proud of you both. Keegan – you are brave, kind, inquisitive, supportive, and empathetic. You are my rock. When the ground shakes around us – you stand firm. Your steadfast conviction and commitment to family inspires me every moment of every day. Colby – you are always my light on the darkest of days. You fill a room with joy, no matter what. You may not have been able to speak your words aloud for many years – but we felt them. And I'm so, so proud of you for finding your voice again, and remaining true to yourself in the process. Thank you for being you. Never let anyone take that away. You are both such kind, compassionate, courageous superheroes. You are so unique, and yet so alike. I love you three thousand.

To my parents, Shirley and Bill Shrieves. You have been my rock since day one. You never stopped believing in me. You never gave up. Not for a moment. In my youth, you were the parents I wish every kid could have. You never missed a game or a performance. You loved me, unconditionally, for me. You've supported me in all the ways. I cannot imagine better parents. You are, and always will be, "home" to me and so many others. And an extra great big shout out for watching the boys for countless hours while I was holed up in my writing studio cranking out *Guided Accountability* and launching Optio. Neither would be possible without you. You guys are the true rock stars here. You win the Unsung Hero award, for sure.

Amanda Seese. Forever my sister, forever my best friend. You were with me in the pits of despair. The lowest of lows. You dropped your entire life and came and cared for my children like they were your own. And when weeks turned into months, you moved them in with you, without hesitation. You were the glue that held my family together that year. Because of you, I'm alive. Because of you, I have a thriving marriage. And because of you, I have two beautiful, healthy children that continue to learn and grow in their innocence. And thank you, Jeff, Makayla, and Destin for rising to meet the challenge. For locking step with my sister and taking the weight of the world on your shoulders. For loving me and my children in the most amazing ways and giving them a "normal" childhood, despite the trauma.

MY MEDICAL TEAM

Franklin Square Hospital, thank you for keeping me alive when all the other hospitals declined.

Thank you to ALL the doctors, nurses, therapists, technicians, and janitorial staff who made it possible for me to be here today to write this book. I'd like to specifically acknowledge a few individuals below who were absolutely essential in my "living" testimony.

Dr. Christopher You, for SEEING me. For being the first surgeon to take me on and not shoo me away, calling me "crazy." For sticking with me every step. And for telling my husband

that every move was not a "Hail Mary" pass when he asked…
even though they all were.

Dr. Stephen Selinger, for being brilliant enough to know that
no one in my situation had ever made it through alive, and
stubborn enough to refuse to accept those odds.

Dr. Avishai Meyer, I thank the universe for bringing you to
the ICU as a traveling surgeon. Your brilliance and your calm
mannerisms were incredibly reassuring, despite the prognosis.

Dr. George Pyrgos, for pushing me to do the impossible. Every day. Even when I really, really didn't want to.

Dr. Stuart Willes, for convincing my husband to put me on
the DNR list for a solid three minutes. In those three minutes,
he realized that was total BS and resolved to do everything
possible to keep me alive. In those three minutes, he realized
I had been fighting this fight so long that he wanted me to
know that if those were to be my last moments, that he had
fought for me all the way to the end, too.

Jennifer Ann, for believing in me every step of the way and
being my champion at every turning point. For refusing to
be removed from my case because you were too emotionally
invested (even though you totally were), and for bringing me
Goodnight Moon to read over FaceTime to my children through
the Passy-Muir Valve in my tracheostomy tube.

Amelia McMahon, for always being my sunflower when the skies were gray.

Terri Ritterpusch, for keeping the team on point.

Gretchen Berry, for not banning my husband from the hospital grounds for putting blue food coloring into my tube feeds to discover where I was leaking.

Jennifer Ihle, I don't know how you cared for me so well when you were in your third trimester – but you were like an angel from above. And thank you for sneaking me extra oxygen when you could.

Nicole Willie, Nicole Henninger, Mike Valetis, Frank Gregoire, Tiffany Sweeney, Nicole Nida, and Billie Simmons for never losing hope.

Henry Wegrocki and Thomas Palm, Jr., thank you for handling all the financial and legal paperwork that needed to happen RIGHT NOW. You guys are the best.

COMMUNITY SUPPORT

Community Christian Church, you will always hold a special place in my heart. Thank you for being our rock in times of great trouble.

Alyce Dailey and The Dailey Group, thank you for organizing all of those who wanted to help. Thank you for the meal chains and the phone trees and believing in me every step of the way.

Mothers of Preschoolers (MOPS), thank you for seeing me. Thank you for hearing me. Thank you for picking up and running with the baton. I wish every woman had a MOPS group as wonderful as you ladies.

Ben Simpkins and our local farm, Richardson's, for feeding my husband every single day so he never had to leave my side. And thank you to ALL the amazing humans who brought food day after day, week after week, especially my family. I am eternally grateful to each and every one of you. And a special shout-out to Ken Adam for showing up so steadily, and never giving up on me.

AT WORK

Thank you to Towson University for their utmost level of understanding when I could not complete a teaching semester.

Dr. Jung-Sook Lee, I would like to thank you, especially, for your never-ending belief in me, and your never-ending patience. You embody every characteristic I've ever longed for in a mentor, and I'm so incredibly lucky to have found you before I even hit my 20s.

83North, you will forever be the most amazing marketing agency to me. Thank you for your patience as my leadership wobbled. Thank you for holding steady the ship in my absence. And an especially great big thank you to the fabulous Todd Pivec, whose patience and support was without end. You, sir, are a good, good man.

Gladys and PJ Gillam, I thank God every day for you both. For your friendship, your wisdom, and your laughter. You were the jet fuel for the Guided Accountability fire in my soul. I'm not sure I would have been brave enough to take off without you both.

Katie and Kevin Barrett, Lisa Bucklin, The Donofrios, Charlie and Sarah Hoehlein, Erin and Jason Ruby, Michelle and Rob Tamburello – thank you for your never-ending support. For sticking with me in ALL of it. For my healing blanket. And for the prayer vigil that may very well have tipped the scales and saved my life. Sarah and Andrew Slattery, a great big thank you for all of the above and also for my most prized physical possession: the shadow box you created with the candles from the vigil. It serves as a constant reminder of how far I've come and how grateful I am for all of you.

PUTTING IT ALL TOGETHER

Lindsey Steel, my soul sister. My original Optio. You have been with me from day one. Your belief in me made it possible to publish this book. If I could wish one thing for the world, it would be for everyone to have their very own Lindsey. How wonderful the world would be then.

Dana Malstaff, the original Boss Mom, I want to thank you for being you. For believing that women can raise both their babies and their businesses well. For being completely brilliant and for leading me on this crazy journey of entrepreneurship. I heart your face, Mama.

Hal Elrod, you have paved the way for so many like me. You have done the undoable. And then, you did it again. And yet you've remained humble, personable…an all-around delightful human being. It is a deep honor to call you "friend."

Selena Soo, my precious PR whisperer. You have taught me so much about interacting with the world at large as an introvert. It has been an absolute delight working so closely with you, and I look forward to many, many more years together.

Nicole Walters, thank you for the Pitch & Pray challenge that encouraged me to get my act together and pull all the pieces together to write this book. I'm so sorry I couldn't go to the Dominican with you, friend. But "Rich Friends are Real Friends"… I'll meet you on the yacht shortly.

Marie Forleo, thank you for believing in me, even when I couldn't. Thank you for seeing me when my vision was off.

Thank you for helping me find my voice in all the noise.

Amy Porterfield, thank you for your love and your loyalty. Thank you for teaching me how to build a team. And thank you for showing me how to go high when they go low. You are such a gem, and I am so, so very thankful

Rachel Hollis – girl, you get me. And I love you for it. Thank you for continuing to show up for me, and for *Guided Account-ability,* month after month. You, my love, are an amazing human.

YOU

Finally, to you, my beloved reader. THANK YOU. Thank you for welcoming me in and allowing me to be a part of your story. I cannot think of a higher honor. Can we stay in touch? Please? I'm always lurking in all the socials: Facebook, Instagram, Twitter, Pinterest, MySpace (just kidding…). But really: please let me know how you're doing, if you found an accountability partner to serve as your guide, and you theirs, and if there is every ANYthing I can do to aide you on this journey and walk alongside you as you become the best, most inspired version of yourself. This movement simply doesn't work without you. I NEED you to put the world back together again, ok? And I deeply honor you for accepting this challenge. Your courage to show up day after day inspires me to show up, too. Okay. Now: I kept this book as short and sweet as possible, so it should still be fresh in your mind. Go out, find a partner, and create the life you deserve, and empower your partner to do the same!

INTRODUCTION

We live in a fast-paced world of shallow relationships. The A-roll of Facebook and Instagram paint distorted pictures of a false reality. You were made for more. You need to drop the 'reel' life of social media and pick up the 'real' life you were meant to live. True connections are forged when we get vulnerable and share our stories and deep emotional experiences with others. The suppression of who we truly are causes comparison, and the side effects are shame and playing small. I'm here to tell you: You were not meant to play small in this world. Your light is meant to shine like a beacon of hope to others struggling in that same false reality. You were born to live in your truth. You are meant to do great things. This is a step-by-step guide to get there.

Throughout this book, I will unveil to you the proven road map to success and provide a tribe of like-minded folks at your back cheering you on. In return, I'm asking three things of you:

1. KEEP READING

I will give you all the tools you need to set goals, accomplish your goals, and bring out success in your partner as well. This community is life-changing and can result in a new state of being. But you have to keep reading to reap the benefits.

2. MAKE THE COMMITMENT

If you commit, this will change the way you appear to yourself, to your Guided Accountability partner (more on that later), to the world, and in your interpersonal relationships. It will allow you to think, exist, and interact as your highest, most inspired, authentic self. It does not mean changing who you are. It means becoming more aware of who you are and having the courage to be vulnerable and show your partner the real you. To get all that awesomeness, you need to make the commitment.

3. CONTINUE TO SHOW UP

I promise you that this system *works*. If you follow this Guided Accountability framework, and just keep taking the next right step, your life will get better than you could have ever imagined. But you have to show up and keep showing up—or you'll miss your best life.

GUIDED ACCOUNTABILITY

THE ROAD MAP

ontrary to the advice of every editor in existence, I'm going to give you the roadmap *first*. Yup, I'm just going to hand over the secret sauce. Why? Because I trust you. And because we can dive in and do the work a heck of a lot faster if we're all starting on the same page.

I'm also a big fan of transparency. So, let me be clear about this. I have spent *a lot* of time, energy, and research developing a system for Guided Accountability called Optio. It's a members-only community in which we bring the pages of this book to life through interactive trainings, including what it means to be a Guided Accountability partner, accessing your personality type through an in-depth assessment, and matching you to your best accountability partner (not your best friend--we're talking the person who's going to bring the best out in you). We then walk you through a 12-week process to define your life's purpose, develop S.M.A.R.T.E.R. goals around that purpose, and figure out how best to get you there through weekly Guided Accountability sessions utilizing our proven framework and private calendar system.

I'm giving you the formula here in these pages to do it yourself because I truly believe in the power of this process and the good it can do in our world. Our algorithms and community make things easier, sure. But you don't *need* our fancy algorithms to take your life to the next level. You can grab this book at your local library, create your own peer group, find your own Guided Accountability partner, and create your own custom Guided Accountability planner/goal tracker based on the prompts in this book. You can do the work and make all your dreams come true. *You* and you alone control your destiny. Just know that we're here as a community of support should you want to take this idea for a test drive in a 'done for you' environment with like-minded peers.

www.myoptio.org

GUIDED ACCOUNTABILITY'S ROAD MAP

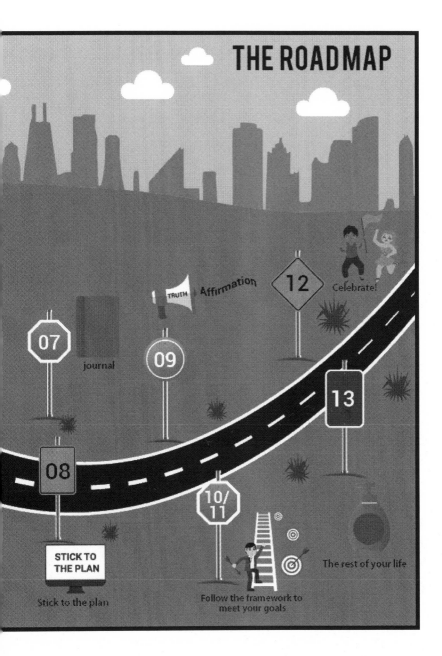

GUIDED ACCOUNTABILITY'S ROAD MAP

1. Identify the personality you're wearing (free 2 question quiz: www.myoptio.org/quick-quiz)
2. Complete your Life Wheel (I've provided a sample and a blank one for you to customize)
3. Set aside 12 weeks to dedicate to becoming the best version of yourself. Make it a priority. Make time for what matters (*You* matter, my friend).
4. Find someone that complements your personality to be your Guided Accountability partner. Make sure they have a copy of this book. You want to choose a partner that is going to challenge you, not just tell you what you want to hear.
5. Come to an agreement/commitment about how you'll support one another (see appendix for sample Guided Accountability contract).
6. Schedule time to meet regularly, face-to-face, once a week for about an hour during these 12 weeks.
7. Start a journal to track your progress (and your partner's progress).
8. Follow the framework provided in the appendix to guide your meeting time. Take turns. One of you will fulfill the role of the guide, leading the other through some well-defined exercises to help reveal their *true* goals (not the goals they *think* they should have). Then you will switch and the guide will become the guided.

You'll follow this process each week for 12 weeks.

9. Week 1: Set affirmations and determine who you will become during this time together.

10. Week 2: Set SMARTER goals

11. Week 3-11: Create milestones to reach these goals. Bring the required traits of a Guided Accountability partner to each session. Adjust as needed.

12. Week 12: Celebrate your successes! Acknowledge your partner. Evaluate the ER portions of your SmartER goals to roll over into your next 12-week sprint.

13. The rest of your life. That's right friends, the evolution never stops. Start again at step one. But guess what? You're a whole new person this time. Your goals are going to get bigger. Your life is going to have more meaning. You'll be living your purpose and your truth, and your whole world is going to change.

Each round of Guided Accountability brings you closer to truly fulfilling your purpose. Guided Accountability is designed to light your soul on fire. You deserve to feel truly alive. No more numbly moving from one season to the next waiting to see what happens to you. Life will no longer happen *to* you. It will forever happen *for* you, my friend.

You're going to design the life you were born to live, a life more amazing than you can imagine. Every 12-week cycle of Guided Accountability opens you up to more and greater possibilities for living out truth in your own life. Peace like you've never known. Confidence that you're living your purpose and that you have the tools and resources to handle whatever opportunities come your way.

When your values are clear, your decisions are easy. Your Guided Accountability partner is going to help you uncover these values, even as the seasons change and values shift (career, family, education, etc.).

Now that we all know where we're going, we can go there together. Let's work through this road map in more detail and improve our lives. Can I get an Amen?

SOME NOTES YOU MAY SEE THROUGHOUT THE BOOK

WHERE YOU MIGHT GET STUCK

I want to be sure to highlight any potential speed bumps on your path. These are not detours by any means, but I want you to be aware of any place you may get stuck, so you don't. Remember: Just keep taking the next right step.

PERSONAL TRIGGERS

We all have things that can push our buttons in ways we might not expect. When this happens, I strongly urge you to reach out to your partner. We are a tribe, a supportive community built on love and mutual respect. We want to see you thrive. Don't be afraid to lean on us—that's what we're here for. It's who we are.

JUST KEEP TAKING THE NEXT RIGHT STEP

This is kind of our motto, Y'all. You'll hear this a lot. I don't have all the answers, and if someone else tells you they do, they're lying—to themselves and to you. Goals and future ways of being can seem intimidating. They can seem far away, distant, unattainable. But if you just keep taking the next right step, I promise you'll get there. Plus, the community will be here to support you when the weight is too great to bear on your own.

CHASE YOUR DREAMS WITH THE DISCIPLINE THEY DESERVE

Too often, we give the best of ourselves to others first. We have to realize that it's true what airline attendants say before take off: We *must* put our own oxygen masks on first before we turn to help others. Otherwise, we will be of no help to anyone at all. Chase your dreams. Chase your passion. Stick to it when it gets hard. When *you* are filled up, your cup will pour over into all those around you. When you let your own light shine, it gives others permission to shine as well.

2

PERSONALITY

In this chapter, I'm going to dive into one of the core pillars that support Guided Accountability's insanely successful framework: Personality. There's a super cool (& *free*) two-question quiz you can take online that will tell you the personality you've been operating in with a 65-percent success rate (come on, y'all… it's *two* questions. Humans are complicated. Sixty-five percent is impressive). You can go there to find out what personality you've been 'wearing' at www.myoptio.org/quick-quiz.

When it comes to Personality, we're going to discuss:

- What personality IS, as it relates to Guided Accountability.
- What personality is NOT: which is just as, if not, *more* important than what it is.
- How to use our own personality (and others') to our common advantage.

Why does personality matter within the Guided Accountability framework?

Identifying and describing our personality provides us with highly specific insights into our psychological and spiritual makeup. Personality helps us by giving us a direction in which to work, but only as long as we remember that it is not telling us who we are, but how we have *limited* who we are.

Let me say that again, because I feel like it's really important here: your personality is not telling you who you are, but how you have *limited* who you are.

Identifying your personality should NOT put you in a box (especially if you're only basing it off that two-question quiz. It's a cool quiz and all, but don't let it limit your sense of self). Identifying the personality you're 'wearing' should show you the box you're already in—and the way out, should you choose to take it.

Let's pull out the therapist card for just a minute. It's a well-known theory that personalities draw upon the capacities of our inborn temperament to develop defenses and compensations to survive and thrive in childhood. In order to get through difficulties and challenges as children, we unwittingly mastered a limited repertoire of strategies, self-images, and behaviors that helped us cope with and thrive in our early environments.

What does that mean for us now, as adults? Well, no matter if you see it as a blessing or a curse, the truth remains that we're faced with *a lot* of decisions as humans. Every day you decide what to eat, when to go to bed, what to wear, even what to say to a stranger at the check-out line (if we say anything at all. Shoot, maybe you ordered from Amazon to avoid that line in the first place). So. Many. Decisions.

That voice in your head that's running a constant monologue is an expression of your personality, and it serves us in *so* many ways. Our lives would be ridiculously complicated without a strong personality to help guide our steps and choices. If we're not careful, it can pigeonhole us, as well. The key is to be in control of your personality and be sure it's serving you, not limiting you.

Now, unlike almost every other thing you've ever heard anyone else say: Optio's Guided Accountability process does *not* approach personality as a hard-wired feature. I see it as the way that you have been choosing to live. But don't worry: even if you believe personality is branded into your DNA: Guided Accountability will still work for you! And remember: no matter what, our personality is only *one* aspect of our very complex and beautiful souls. Although being aware of the personality we are wearing is important and helpful in many ways, it is important to note that we are *much more* than our personalities. Our personalities are no more than the familiar, conditioned parts of a much wider range of potential that we all possess. We're going to unleash a lot of them in these chapters.

Guided Accountability's purpose is not to help you get rid of your personality. That wouldn't be very helpful. I already outlined how our personalities help us navigate through life. The reason we identify our personality is for it to become more transparent and flexible: something that helps us live rather than something that takes over our lives. Leverage your personality to empower you, but don't use it as an excuse. It is important to realize we are *not* our personality. To begin to grasp this is to undergo a transformation of your sense of self. When you begin to understand that we are not our personalities, we also begin to realize that we are spiritual beings who *have* a personality. Big difference, guys. *Big.*

WHY LOOK AT PERSONALITY AT ALL FOR GUIDED ACCOUNTABILITY?

When you have identified the personality you are wearing, it allows for incredible insights. You will be able to discover how to best leverage your body's automatic responses to certain life situations.

DON'T GET STUCK: Personality is just a small part of us that is easy to compartmentalize and leverage. It's always good to know when you have leverage, and how to get it when you don't. Guided Accountability is not intended for you to use your personality to dictate what you do with your life. We use personality as a tool to empower potential, not limit it.

Once you've identified the personality you're wearing, you can observe and let go of the habits and mechanisms of your personality that have trapped you, then learn to secure and lean into the habits and mechanisms that have brought you strength and served you well.

When looking for your ideal Guided Accountability partner, you want to take *their* personalities into account as well. Now this might hurt, but hear me out: You do *not* want your Guided Accountability partner to be your best friend. You want your Guided Accountability partner to bring out the best in you, and that is a different animal entirely. It's a unique relationship built on complementary characteristics, like puzzle pieces. You fit together, but you're *not* the same. *Together,* you make a greater whole.

Finding the perfect Guided Accountability partner doesn't let you off the hook, they just get you where you're going *faster*. We continue to push forward in our own personal development through personality insights. Your level of success will rarely exceed your personal development, because your success is something you attract by the person you become. Never place limits on your potential, and don't let anyone else place limits on you. If you're curious how to shatter that glass ceiling you've placed over your own head, read on.

3

START
WHERE YOU ARE
WITH THE LIFE WHEEL

L ife can be crazy busy. I know. That's the very reason Guided Accountability came to be. It's easy to allow all of your energy to be absorbed by one particular project or focused on one specific task. It's easy to get so wrapped up in one facet of life that you neglect other areas, some of which are really important for your long-term health, success, and well-being.

So when we approach Guided Accountability, we start where we are. We take an honest inventory of our lives and see where we're at. How? The Life Wheel.

Commonly used by top professional coaches and therapists,

The Life Wheel allows you to reflect and gain some insight into the balance of your life and how satisfied you are in life's different areas. It allows you to press pause and take a "helicopter view" of your life as it is right now, in *this* season.

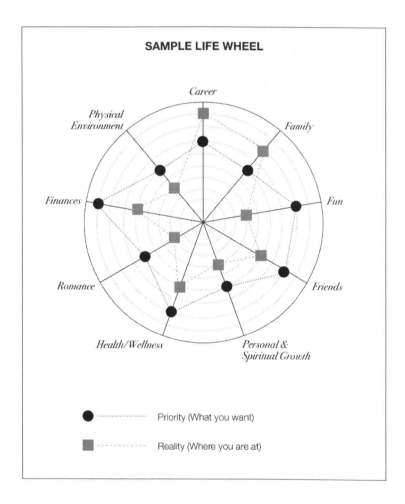

SAMPLE LIFE WHEEL

Career
Physical Environment
Family
Finances
Fun
Romance
Friends
Health/Wellness
Personal & Spiritual Growth

● ·············· Priority (What you want)

■ - - - - - Reality (Where you are at)

The Life Wheel is a great tool for helping you begin your journey by creating more balance, happiness, and success in your life. It is a great foundational exercise when goal-setting or establishing your focus. Using this tool, you will be able to reflect and gain some insight into the *balance* of your life and how satisfied you are in life's different areas.

Take an honest inventory of your life and evaluate where you are with regard to each category. This is a constantly evolving inventory. Once you evaluate where you are, in this moment, you can further delve into *why* your Life Wheel looks the way it does, what you really want it to look like, and how to make this change happen with your Guided Accountability partner.

Why do we do this? There's no doubt that drive and focus are requirements when it comes to getting things done, but narrowing your focus too far can lead to frustration and intense stress. This can often leave us wondering why everything feels so "off." That's when it's time to take a step back and bring things into balance.

I've included a sample Life Wheel with life areas that represent a large portion of Optio's members. Feel free to use those same categories for yourself, or customize at your discretion on the blank Life Wheel provided.

Here's how to make the Life Wheel your own:

1. BRAINSTORM LIFE AREAS

Maybe your wheel represents the roles you play in life. For example: wife/husband/partner, mother/father/Guardian, manager, community leader, daughter/son, sister/brother, friend, etc.

Or your wheel may represent areas of life that are important to you. For example: career, education, family, friends, finances, health, etc.

Your wheel might even be your own unique combination of both. Bottom line: the Life Wheel should represent a well rounded, eagle's-eye view of what a successful and balanced version of *your life* and *your priorities* look like as they stand in this season. Your Life Wheel should reflect *your* values. Because when your values are clear, your decisions are easy.

2. NARROW DOWN YOUR SELECTIONS

Once you've narrowed down your selections, write an area on each of the spokes on the Life Wheel.

3. ASSESS EACH AREA

This approach assumes that you will be happy and fulfilled if you can find the right balance of attention for each of these dimensions. Different areas of your life will need different levels of attention at different times and in different seasons, so the next step is to assess the amount of attention you're currently devoting to each area. Take an honest inventory of your life and evaluate where you are with regard to each category.

There is a scoring system behind using the Wheel where you simply reflect and rate your satisfaction levels out of 10, where 1 is closest to the center of the circle and 10 is at the edge of the circle.

Consider each dimension in turn, and on a scale of 0 (low) to 10 (high), write down the amount of attention you're devoting to that area of your life. Mark each score on the appropriate spoke of your Life Wheel.

4. CONNECT THE DOTS

Now join up the marks around the circle. Does your life wheel look and feel balanced? It's OK if it doesn't: that's what we're here for.

5. THINK ABOUT YOUR IDEAL LEVEL

Next, it's time to consider your ideal level in each area of your life. A balanced life does not mean getting a 5 in each life area: some areas need more attention and focus than others at any time. Inevitably you will need to make choices and compromises, as your time and energy are not in unlimited supply!

Balance—*true* Balance—is bogus. Parenting children means they're going to fall at a higher level on your Life Wheel at 30 days than they will at 30 years (or so we hope). The idea of 'balance' is going to change, but what's important is to align your values and your time. If you're living in your purpose, everything else will flow far more easily.

So the question is, what would the ideal level of attention be for you in each life area?

Plot the "ideal" scores around your life wheel and, again, connect the dots.

(I recommend using a different color to jazz it up and help differentiate your wants versus the reality.)

6. TAKE ACTION

Now you have a visual representation of your current life balance and your ideal life balance. Where are the gaps? These are the areas of your life that need attention.

Remember that gaps go both ways. There are almost certainly areas that are not getting as much attention as you'd like. However, there may also be areas where you're putting in *more* effort than you'd like. These areas are sapping energy and enthusiasm that may be better directed elsewhere.

Once you have identified the areas that need your attention, it's time to plan the actions needed to work on regaining balance. Concerning your neglected areas, what things do you need to do to regain balance? In the areas that currently sap too much of your energy and time, what can you stop doing, re-prioritize, or delegate to someone else? Make note of these revelations and roll over these ideas and concepts. You're going to put them to great use in the upcoming stages.

THE CATEGORIES ON THE WHEEL ARE JUST A SUGGESTION.

Essentially, the Life Wheel is divided into different categories of life that are important to you. What's suggested here are the common categories Optio members encounter in day-to-day life. You will find that with the provided Life Wheel, you will be able to score yourself in the majority of key areas in your life.

However, before you rush into it and complete the Wheel, you may want to think about the categories themselves, their application to your life, and whether or not there are other categories that make sense for you to evaluate in this season. Feel free to adjust the suggested categories so that they accurately evaluate your life in this season. If there are alternative categories you'd like to include, customize the wheel to suit your particular lifestyle—but be sure to share this information with your Guided Accountability partner so he or she can include it in the weekly inquiry. I have provided a template that can be customized to fit your current season below.

IT'S JUST A GUT CHECK. Your response is based entirely on how YOU feel you are doing in a certain category. It's objective, and you call all the shots. There really aren't any wrong answers, so just enjoy the ride.

LIFE IS LIKE RIDING A BICYCLE. To keep your balance, you must keep moving. True Balance is more like juggling than balancing. You want to keep the balls in the air—but you can't be fully focused on all of them all the time. You need to let some go in order to embrace others. Just keep moving forward. Just keep taking the next right step.

CUSTOMIZE YOUR LIFE WHEEL

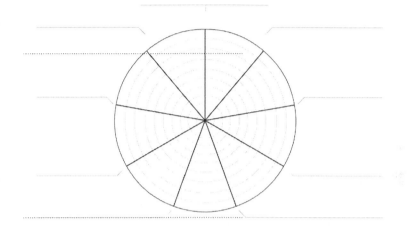

The Life-Wheel is a great tool to help you improve your life balance. Whether you create your own or leverage Optio's: It helps you quickly and graphically identify the areas in your life to which you want to devote more energy and helps you understand where you might want to cut back. The challenge now is to transform this knowledge and desire for a more balanced life into a positive program of action. Feel free to fill in the areas of the pie above in a way that reflects your own life in this season.

4

ACCOUNTABILITY

Now that we've discovered a bit about *who* and *where* you are in this season of life, it's time to dive into the concept of Accountability. In this chapter, I'm going to talk about what accountability *is* and what it *isn't*. I'll also provide you with some tips and tricks for successfully engaging in accountability.

WHAT IS ACCOUNTABILITY?

There are quite a few definitions of accountability floating around in the universe, so I want to nail this one down for you as it pertains to our Guided Accountability framework:

ACCOUNTABILITY IS THE ACT OF BEING RESPONSIBLE TO SOME-ONE ELSE FOR SOME ACTION OR RESULT; TO ACCOUNT FOR YOUR ACTIVITIES, ACCEPT RESPONSIBILITY FOR THEM, AND DISCLOSE THE RESULTS TO ANOTHER IN A TRANSPARENT MANNER.

Accountability is answerability, and expectation of account-giving. Very little happens in the world, or in your life, without some form of accountability. Accountability aims to improve both the internal standard of individual and group conduct as well as external factors, such as sustainable habit improvements and goal tracking. Accountability involves either the expectation or assumption of account-giving behavior. Accountability doesn't happen just by chance; it has to be implemented and opted into. Accountability is a *choice*.

This next section might be a bit intimidating, but you really need to understand the role *you* play in accountability.

Accountability means letting go of the victim mentality for good and embracing that *you* have power over your own life. This is a really important concept to grab hold of. Our Guided Accountability framework does not work if you're not holding yourself accountable for your own choices. Only *you* have the power to make changes in your world. No one else. Own your power.

ACCOUNTABILITY STARTS WITH YOU

Participants of the Guided Accountability movement define our culture, and if we want to create a culture of accountability (and believe me: we do) then it starts with you.

To start: I need you to model the behaviors that you want to see in your partner and understand their expectations of you. Unfortunately, the golden rule, "Do unto others as you would have them do unto you," is intrinsically flawed. What we *really* need to do is *listen* to what others expect from us and need from us, and do *that*.

As your original source for Guided Accountability, we promise to own our part and be sure all systems are in place to take pressure off your shoulders. But, you need to show up if you want that. You have to take ownership. When you make this commitment, you have to keep this commitment. If you don't, you will stop motivating your partner, and you will stop motivating yourself.

— — — — — — — — — — —

WE'LL PAVE THE ROAD: but *you* need to walk (not just talk) the accountability path.

— — — — — — — — — — —

As an accountability partner, you are accountable. You're accountable for any failures, as well as any successes, that your partnership achieves. Accountability comes as part of the job description, which is why, if you try to duck it, responsibility will have a negative impact on the levels of accountability that already exist.

ACCOUNTABILITY IS NOT A ONE-TIME THING

Accountability is an *all-time* thing. It's a lifestyle choice. Not a diet. Those who don't want to be held accountable are always looking for an opportunity to get out of it. Any gaps in your accountability will give them the out they need.

That's not you. That's why you're here. To become the best version of yourself, you need to be accountable at all times.

That doesn't mean you never fail; quite the contrary. What it *does* mean is that you own your failures, learn great things from them, improve, and move on. You don't do amazing things in this world without a few failures. You don't do amazing things in this world if you don't take responsibility for your actions.

ACCOUNTABILITY APPLIES TO ONE AND ALL

When you're looking to hold people accountable, you cannot play favorites. You cannot "let it slide" with certain partners. This is why you should do some research to determine the best Guided Accountability partner *for you*, or allow Optio's algorithm to do the matching work for you. Your Guided Accountability partner is *not* your best friend (sorry, not sorry). This person is more like a missing puzzle piece. His or her jagged edges round out your softer ones and vice versa. You want to choose a partner you are capable of challenging, and who can be expected to challenge you.

ACCOUNTABILITY IS CONSISTENT

That's what you're here for. Consistency leads to greatness.

ACCOUNTABILITY CANNOT BE DELEGATED

You simply have to accept it and take ownership. Be sure your accountability partner has *chosen* this path of accountability, too. Willingly. They need to desire the best life possible for themselves and for you. The best way to get individuals to accept accountability is to set them up to be successful. That's exactly where Guided Accountability comes in, and what we have done with our process. We've set you both up for success. We've paved the path. You just need to walk it, and start leaning into the idea of success. You're going to see a lot more of it from now on.

If you want your partner to accept accountability (and you do), be sure he or she has everything they need to be successful. If he doesn't, then find out what he needs to feel confident. Create space to identify what she needs to actualize her success, and brainstorm possible ways to get there. When he accepts accountability, he has taken a big step toward accepting Guided Accountability.

ACCOUNTABILITY IS THE DIFFERENCE BETWEEN SUCCESS AND FAILURE

When people don't take accountability and things start to go awry, they don't feel ownership over their lives. They go into spectator mode and watch as things fail. You've seen the fans in the stands, blaming the coach or another player. If they thought it would fail from the outset it nearly always becomes a self-fulfilling prophecy, which is even worse. Then they go into "I told you so" mode. This is why truly believing our affirmations is so important.

The good news is that when we take ownership, we step into solution mode when things start to go wrong. We try to figure out what's going wrong, then try to fix it. Automatically. Like breathing. Successful partnerships are full of people that go into solution mode. They are full of people who not only care but take care. Accountability is the single biggest differentiator between successful and unsuccessful teams and individuals.

ACCOUNTABILITY IS A DISCIPLINE

Prioritize your Guided Accountability appointments. By creating integrity around your meeting time, you're allowing several things:

- It lets them know they will be held accountable for their activities.
- It gives you an opportunity to provide them support in case things start to go awry.
- It offers you the opportunity to offer praise and encouragement to move your partner further along if things are going well.

WHERE YOU MIGHT GET STUCK. Accountability is something that has to be worked at. We've provided a clear and consistent strategy for how to implement it. You just need to keep taking the next right step. It's important to keep in mind that Guiding is NOT about projecting perceived wrongs on our partners. Guided Accountability does not include lecturing. Approach accountable conversations with humility, saying, "I see great potential in you, and you can be more than you are today."

Remember, when you take on the role as a Guide it's not about *you*. It's about your Guided Accountability *partner*.

YOU HAVE TO 'SHOW UP' FOR YOUR PARTNER

Accountability starts with you, and it has to apply at all times and to everyone. When you stop showing up, things fall apart.

BONUS: YOU WILL BEGIN 'SHOWING UP' FOR YOURSELF IN A WAY YOU NEVER IMAGINED.

When you hold yourself and your partner accountable, you help create a culture of accountability. Your individual accountability will allow Guided Accountability to hold the expectation of accountability for the movement at large (shew—that was a lot of "accountability"s). When an entire community shows up in authentic ways, taking responsibility for themselves and their world, amazing things happen.

Every time you choose to do the easy thing instead of the right thing, you are shaping your identity, becoming the type of person who does what's easy, rather than what's right. Let's build a community of people that continuously choose to do the right thing, together.

The choices you make today, the actions you take, determine who you become. It is who you become (not just what you do) that will determine both the quality and the direction of the rest of your life. You are, in this moment, exactly where you are meant to be. Even if it's hard, it's a journey. You don't need to take on all of life at once. Just keep taking the next right step.

5

GUIDED
ACCOUNTABILITY

Let's switch gears. I've established what it means to be accountable, but what about what it means to be a Guide? Let's start with the definition, shall we?

A GUIDE IS ONE THAT LEADS OR DIRECTS ANOTHER'S WAY; ONE WHO PROVIDES ANOTHER WITH GUIDING INFORMATION. A GUIDE IS CHARGED WITH STEADYING OR DIRECTING THE MOTION OF SOMETHING.

Bottom line: When performing in the role of 'Guide,' you are holding your accountability partner responsible for today's actions and tomorrow's commitments.

SO: WHAT IS GUIDED ACCOUNTABILITY? I've defined the pieces separately, but what do they mean when they're combined? What IS "Guided Accountability"?

GUIDED ACCOUNTABILITY IS THE PROCESS BY WHICH ONE OR MORE PARTICIPANTS SET GOALS IN RESPONSE TO GUIDANCE PROVIDED BY A PARTNER. PARTICIPANTS ARE THEN HELD ACCOUNTABLE IN MEETING THOSE GOALS BY SAID PARTNER.

It seems simple, and it *is*! And it isn't.

It's like going to the gym. You know it's good for you, and it's the right thing to do, but showing up again and again is hard! Simple in concept, more challenging in execution. That's where the framework comes in. Left-brained friends, this may help break down Guided Accountability for you.

Let's go back to grade-school math and science. Are you still with me? If you checked out during math and science, just hear me out.

Like the mathematical term, Vector, Guided Accountability can be represented by an arrow, composed of both direction and magnitude (and yes, *Despicable Me* fans, I totally stole that. No shame in my mom game). The accountable party holds the magnitude, the guide provides direction, or space for an intentional direction to be explored.

Now think back to science lab. Develop a hypothesis for the trajectory of your life. A hypothesis is used to define the relationship between two variables. A *variable* is any item, factor, or condition that can be controlled or changed. Can you change the passing of time? Einstein's Relativity aside, no—and odds are, If you are reading this book, you are probably not on a spaceship traveling near the speed of light.

For our purposes, time is constant. But *how you choose to spend that time* is up to you. Our quality of life is the variable. When are you going to decide that your life is a variable worth investing in?

If I've lost you, my right-brained friends, no worries. Here's an image to help break it down for your creative, picture-driven souls.

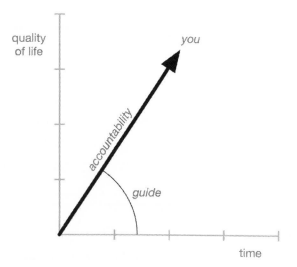

Guiding isn't difficult, but you've been trained for years to avoid it, so you may be a little rusty. Frankly, you're probably a little uncomfortable having a conversation that looks like those that occur in the Guided Accountability space. They sometimes require space for silence, deeper thought, uncomfortable questions, and mirroring what you see, not just what you think the other person wants to hear.

I'm here to help you realize that you already have all the skills you need to make a huge difference in your partner's life. I want to sell you on that idea, because your partner's success depends on you understanding that you must be responsible as their accountability partner. I need you to show up, but *just* showing up isn't sufficient. I need you to *truly* show up. Be there, be in the moment. I need you to be present and give all of yourself for their growth. Listen. Give them the space they need that is so hard to find in this busy, demanding world. You can also expect *them* to be present for *you* and give you this same space. Are you starting to see what a gift that could be?

If you're starting to wonder why you can't just carve this space out for yourself, I'd encourage you to consider that the true value of a guide is to serve as a mirror to the guided, to point out blind spots you may not be aware of and strengths that may have gone underappreciated.

The Guided Accountability framework walks you through every step of the way. We have literally outlined the exact conversations you need to have for all 12 weeks of your Guided Accountability commitment (see appendix). Twelve weeks is not an arbitrary or random time commitment. It's based on a significant amount of science, data, and research that shows that when we truly push ourselves, we get the MOST return on our investments within a 12-week cycle (check out the reading list at the end of this book to see some of the many researchers that paved the way for us to blaze THIS path for you). We have structured this time and space to allow you and your partner to get the absolute most out of your time together. This pairing is about *connection,* and you have what it takes—inside you right now, in this very moment—to guide your partner to see amazing results.

— — — — — — — — — — — —

Guides often lead participants through the framework to engage in visualization and mental imagery generation that may simulate or recreate the sensory perception of sights, sounds, tastes, smells, movements, and images. The generating of such mental imagery can precipitate or accompany strong emotions or feelings. This framework highlights both positive and negative imagery that comes up for the partner with regard to certain areas of the Life Wheel. It sheds light on limiting beliefs we may have about ourselves as well as stories that we've been told (or told to ourselves) over time that may not be entirely based in truth. It also sheds light on untapped strengths and traits that can be leveraged for growth.

— — — — — — — — — — —

The Guided Accountability framework often encourages participants to document their experience, most commonly in the form of a self-reflective journal or diary. These Guide Sheets are simply meant to create an outline for that lead in discussion. A full Guided Accountability Planner is available if you are looking for a proven way to keep yourself on track.

It's important to note that guides are *not* therapists or coaches, though it may feel like they are. Guides are simply asking questions provided through the Guided Accountability framework and holding space for the guided to make their own discoveries. They are not meant to solve problems or give answers.

— — — — — — — — — — —

PROGRESS. NOT PERFECTION. You know our motto: just keep taking the next right step. This whole process is about progress, not perfection.

— — — — — — — — — — —

If you're not uncomfortable, you're not reaching your potential. Seriously: If you're not uncomfortable at some point in these Guided Accountability sessions (both as the guide and the guided), it's almost certain that you're not reaching your potential. You're holding back. When you start to feel uncomfortable, live in those feelings. You're not stuck. You're progressing.

— — — — — — — — — — — —

Guided Accountability provides you with a safe space to GET OUT OF YOUR COMFORT ZONE. Use it.

— — — — — — — — — — — —

This brings us to a few characteristics you're going to want to develop and/or strengthen as you walk the journey of Guided Accountability. This will happen naturally, but if you intentionally pursue their growth, you can make it happen far more quickly.

- **DISCIPLINE:** Just keep taking the next right step. You choose discipline when you engage in the consistent pattern of showing up. Some days you may not feel like showing up and doing the work. Discipline is the assertion of willpower over more basic desires. Just keep showing up.

- **INTEGRITY:** Do the right thing. You're leveraging discipline and showing up to your Guided Accountability sessions consistently and on time. Be *truly* present: pay attention and listen to your partner. Stay focused. Don't allow yourself to be distracted by "life." Your partner deserves your full attention and you, theirs. Give it freely and take responsibility for your end of the Guided Accountability relationship.

- **VULNERABILITY:** I'm going to encourage you right now to embrace your vulnerability as your strength. It is through this vulnerability that you will grow exponentially. Vulnerability is the lifesource of all good things in this world. Hope, empathy, accountability, and authenticity are all sourced from vulnerability. Vulnerability is the key to unlocking your true potential through Guided Accountability.

- **GRATITUDE:** You'll never get more of what you want until you're truly grateful for what you have. Incorporate a gratitude practice into your daily life. The benefits are endless. You'll feel more alive and positive in your space. You'll sleep better. You'll express more compassion, kindness, and empathy. You'll even boost your immune system. Just do it.

6

BUT DOES IT WORK?

I want to take a moment to truly acknowledge your effort and grit in making it this far. You are proving to me and our community at large that you are in it to win it. A true Guided Accountability partner at heart. I'm so glad you're still here with me.

Now let's talk about whether or not this process actually works in the real world (Spoiler Alert: IT DOES!). Let's dive into the nitty-gritty. The facts. The evidence. Let's get real about what kind of results you can expect through Guided Accountability. Math/science friends: you asked for the data, and I have some seriously amazing statistics to back up this proven process. Buckle up, or you'll get blown away.

You're skeptical. I get it. When I started this project, I was skeptical, too. Could this actually work the way I envisioned it? Could this really change individual lives and communities at large one conversation at a time? Indeed it can, and indeed it *does*.

Here's what I've learned.

The American Society of Training and Development (ASTD) did a study on accountability and found that you have a 65-percent greater chance of completing a goal if you commit to someone. That, alone, is an impressive increase in results. But they also proved that using Optio's Guided Accountability framework—having a specific accountability appointment with a person you've committed to—will increase your chances of success by 95 percent.

Here's the ASTD's breakdown:

The rise in probability of completing a goal if:
- You *have* an idea or a goal: 10%
- You *consciously decide* you will do it: 25%
- You decide *when* you will do it: 40%
- You *plan how* you will do it: 50%
- You *commit to someone* you will do it: 65%
- You have a *specific accountability appointment* with a person you've committed to: 95%

The Guided Accountability framework takes the proven accountability process even further. We recommend partners based on your personality type, AND we've created a step-by-step process and worksheet to walk you through each of the twelve weeks.

If these results sound too good to be true, I challenge you to test the theory. Give Guided Accountability all you've got. Show up. Commit. See what happens. You have everything to gain, and nothing to lose. It's a win-win.

— — — — — — — — — — — —

If you find these statistics a little overwhelming: you're not alone. When presented with results like these, many of us immediately discount them, mainly because we're afraid (even if we haven't recognized that yet). What if I fail? What does that mean for me? If everyone else is achieving a 95-98 percent success rate, and I fail, what does that say about ME? But here's the thing: You CAN'T fail. Not really. Because no matter what, you'll be held up and supported by a community that understands exactly where you are and wants to help you be the best, most inspired version of yourself, no matter where you are on the journey. We have a motto I think you might like: Fail Frequently. Fail Fast. Fail Forward. THAT is how we win!

— — — — — — — — — — — —

And we win through community! The Guided Accountability

community has formed an incredibly supportive tribe. Tribes become extremely actionable as a result of the strong bond formed between members of the group. When members of the tribe commit to being open, honest, and accountable with each other, the acceleration of individual growth for each member is powerful. Just imagine it. With an entire community of successful individuals pushing you forward, what could you do? It's time to start shedding those limiting beliefs, friends. It's time to start owning your power.

7

AFFIRMATIONS

By now I hope you're getting the sense that this Guided Accountability community is pretty darn powerful. A movement comprised of the most amazing individuals this world has to offer, called to the highest purpose. We plan to move the needle for world peace with the powerful collective force of personal responsibility and Guided Accountability. United, we are a seriously powerful force. Collectively, our voices cannot go unheard. Now it's time to get into the nuts and bolts of Guided Accountability. The HOW. Our affirmations and goal setting.

This isn't woo-woo, friends. This is science. I'll define affirmations as they apply to Guided Accountability and talk about how they help us plot our course. I'll also talk about truly effective goal creation. You may have a system that you love for goal tracking and creation, and if that's the case, GREAT. For the rest of us that could use a little help staying on track, I have an amazing, foolproof process to get you up and running, and all the way to the finish line in record time.

— — — — — — — — — — —

Remember: Guided Accountability isn't just about blasting through your goals. It's about enjoying the process and the journey. The relationships. After all, life is what happens when you're busy making plans, right?

— — — — — — — — — — —

AFFIRMATIONS

You may have been using affirmations since you were old enough to form conscious thought, or, like me, you may not have been introduced to the idea of affirmations until late in adulthood (if ever at all). Well, we're about to change that. I encourage you to keep an open mind—this is powerful stuff, friends, but it's only powerful if you let it be, so stop right now and make a commitment to get out of your own way!

According to the *English American Dictionary*, to "affirm" is to state that something is true.

Within the Guided Accountability community, an affirmation is a statement of truth which one aspires to absorb into his or her life. Affirmations are dynamic and practical, not just wishful thinking. One reason they work is because they are based on truths that we have yet to realize on a conscious level. One of the greatest mistakes we make as humans is not recognizing our own power to change ourselves into the people we want to be. When done correctly, the repetition of affirmations and the corresponding mental images formed when saying them help to change the subconscious mind.

Ideally, affirmations should be repeated in a quiet space with concentration. This repetition allows you to change habit patterns and attitudes over things you may typically feel little to no control. That's right, control freaks, I'm giving you control over the uncontrollable. You can thank me later.

NEED SOME EXAMPLES?

Here are just a few of the affirmations that the Guided Accountability community have leveraged in their 12-week programs and brought into regular rotation in their lives.

- I have the ability to change the world through the work I do
- I follow my intuition and my heart; keeping me safe and sound
- I make the right choices every time

- I trust myself
- I am the master of my wealth
- Wonderful things unfold before me
- I surround myself with people who treat me well
- Life happens FOR me.

Your Guided Accountability partner will walk you through the process of constructing your own relevant, impactful affirmation to guide your quarter using the first weekly worksheet.

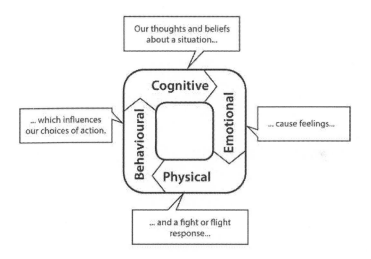

This is seriously powerful stuff, guys. Trust me. Let the universe do its thing.

I know it kind of sounds like woo-woo, but it's legit. There are loads of science to back it up. I don't want to get *too* technical, but basically, your subconscious has the power to create a new reality for your dominant consciousness. Words are the conduit between the emotions we feel and the thoughts we think.

Who doesn't want to leverage their own super power? This is doubly powerful when you merge your subconscious brain with your physiology. What do I mean by that? Create a gesture that goes with your affirmation. I strongly suggest looking up the American Sign Language for your affirmation. Then create an abbreviated or slang version of that sign language. But it doesn't have to be ASL. It can be as simple as tapping your thigh or squeezing your left palm three times every time you say your affirmation. The goal is to create a mental and physical connection, which doubles the potency. It's about hacking our bodies and minds.

— — — — — — — — — — —

LET GO OF FEELING SILLY. I get it. The first couple weeks I embraced affirmations, I felt completely ridiculous. Talking to myself in the bathroom mirror. Talking to myself in the car. Signing 'slang' when no one was looking. And the *most* uncomfortable part? Sharing my affirmation with my partner and having *them* tell *me* who I was. UGH! It felt like squeamish torture. But then, something happened: the affirmations that seemed so far from reality started to seem achievable. Suddenly, they were simply truth. Now I realize that if I have a super power to control my own destiny, I don't really care about feeling silly getting there. Everyone else should feel silly for *not* embracing their potential. Just sayin'.

— — — — — — — — — — — —

Even Muhammad Ali got it. He shouted affirmations to himself every day. *Shouted* them. *Every* day. When you think of Muhammad Ali, I'm guessing 'silly' isn't the first adjective that comes to mind.

"It's the repetition of affirmations that leads to belief. Once that belief becomes a deep conviction, things begin to happen." – Muhammad Ali

8

GOALS:
REDEFINE
WHAT'S POSSIBLE

O nce you've sculpted your affirmation, you'll begin creating and meeting goals that get you there faster.

There are loads of ways to set goals. If you've been around the goal-setting block a few times, you may be familiar with a few of these: MBO, OGSM, KPI, OKR, Sprint Goals, Scrum Goal setting, SMART goals, CLEAR goals, HARD goals, ACTION goal setting, EXACT goal setting, FRAME goal setting, QUEST goal setting, SUCCESS goal setting, FABRIC goal setting, PRAGMATIC goal setting, even DUMB goal setting (yes, it's a real thing. There are even three different and widely distributed variants of the DUMB goals acronym. You can't make this stuff up).

Or maybe this is all just alphabet soup to you.

If you're starting to break out into hives thinking I'm going to ask you to take on a different standard for goal setting when you think you have one pretty down pat, don't sweat it. If you are passionate about a certain goal-setting method, and it's worked for you, *keep doing it*. I'm not here to fix what's not broken.

Whether you choose to take on Guided Accountability's goal framework or not, I DO encourage you to consider these tips within your Guided Accountability pairing:

1. No matter how experienced you are, lean into your guide and your Life Wheel.
2. Always set goals that motivate you, and which apply to:
   a. Your life
   b. Your dreams

REMEMBER YOUR WHY. The WHY behind the goal is even more important than the actualization of the goal itself. Like Simon Sinek says: "Start with Your Why." (If you don't know Simon Sinek, his five-minute TEDtalk is worth giving a whirl.)

Keep your why and your Life Wheel at the forefront of your

mind. Let your *values* dictate your goals because who you are becoming by reaching for these goals is even more important than what you are actually doing. What you do determines who you become. Let that sink in. Talk about a win-win.

Guided Accountabilities Gold Standard for Goal setting:

S.M.A.R.T.E.R.

Within the Guided Accountability community, we support S.M.A.R.T.E.R. goals.

- **SPECIFIC:** Be clear about what you want to accomplish. If you don't know exactly where you want to go, how will you know when you get there?

- **MEASURABLE:** Include precise amounts, dates, numbers, etc. General terms leave too much wiggle room in your goal setting.

- **ATTAINABLE:** Make sure your goals are possible. This is the part where dreamers start to buck the system a bit. Don't limit your goal setting to what you've *seen* as possible. We are all human. It can be difficult to aim for a goal we cannot see. Yet by reaching for the unreachable, we truly disrupt the system and can create great and powerful change. Overall: attainable, yes. But keep pushing those boundaries, friends. Just because you haven't seen it doesn't mean it can't happen.

- **RELEVANT:** Make sure your goals are in alignment with your affirmation, which is in alignment with your values. Your goals should take you in the direction of who you want to be. Your affirmation sculpts this beautifully at the beginning of your quarter. Be sure your goals (long-term and the milestones in between) fall in line and are consistent with this version of yourself.

- **TIME-BOUND:** Your goals must have a deadline. Guided Accountability pairings run in 12-week sprints, which is the proven time allocation for the most productivity with the least amount of burn out. A lot of research went into this system, friends. *Work the system.*

- **EVALUATE:** Throughout your 12 weeks, continually evaluate what is pushing you toward your goals. What's working? What's not? Then have a really intentional evaluation at the end of the 12 weeks. Did you meet your goal? Evaluate why you *did* or why you did *not*. Learning from each of these scenarios is equally important. Remember: Fail frequently. Fail fast. Fail forward. You can only do that if you're evaluating each failure.

- **READJUST:** It's OK to adjust your goals. If you realize mid-sprint that you're running in the wrong direction, don't keep sprinting just because you said you would. *Readjust.* If a pilot took off from California heading to NYC, but their angle was off by a degree or two, where do you think they'd end up? Readjust, friends. There's no shame in the readjustment game. Believe me.

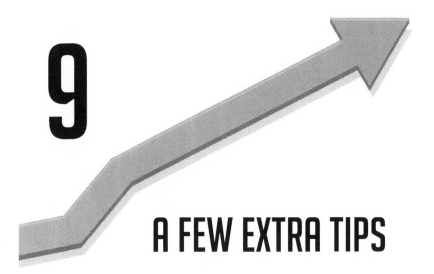

9

A FEW EXTRA TIPS

- Get your goals down in writing, preferably with a pen and paper. Don't just *talk* it out with your partner--*write* your goals in your weekly sheets. I didn't design them for my health.

- Make an action plan. There's a reason you meet weekly to be sure you don't fall too far off the path. If you do, take corrective measures in time to, you know, correct!

- Stick with it! If you don't make your goals one week, that is all the *more* reason to *get on that call*. That's what accountability is all about. Get back on that horse. Minimize your derailments.

- *Truly* turn your SMART goals into SMART – ER – goals. When you roll over into your next quarter with a new accountability partner, roll along with you an EVALUATION of the goals you set the prior quarter. How did you do? Did you meet every goal? If so, should you be shooting bigger? If not, what can you do to get there this quarter with your new partner? And READJUST. There's a reason we encourage you to change Guided Accountability partners every 12 weeks. Each partner allows for readjustment. You can't get too comfortable in your way of doing things or with your view of the world. Every partner gives you a window into the world's unseen, and a culture you haven't experienced. Every partner brings with them their own unique wisdom that will allow you to expand your thinking process and encourage you to READJUST your goals with new eyes.

- Creating goals can be intimidating, especially goals that someone is going to be holding you accountable for down the road. Don't let this hold you back. It's OK if you don't meet your goals. It's about progress. Not perfection.

- Just keep taking the next right step, and you can't go

wrong. You've got this. Setting goals is the first step in turning the invisible visible. You can't go somewhere you can't see. Clear goals, attached to a specific vision, allow you to chart the course to what you may have previously thought to be impossible. Dream big, friends, and Goal Get 'Em.

10

AFTERWORD: WHERE TO FIND US FOR MORE HELP

EXPECTATIONS OF THE GUIDED ACCOUNTABILITY COMMUNITY

I'm about to get really clear on what is expected of an active Guided Accountability pairing and what we ask of the community at large. I'm also going to walk you through a process to do this entirely on your own, as well as how to join a membership community that does all the heavy lifting for you.

First things first: The level of commitment is up to you, but Guided Accountability only works if you opt in—if you *choose* to be accountable to your specific partner.

If you choose to just engage in the community and not work with a specific accountability partner yet, that is A-OK. Dip your toes in the water. See what it's all about. We welcome you to engage in social media and follow along as our community grows. We expect you to honor, respect, and elevate the group with your contributions. Diverse opinions are welcome. The most personal growth occurs when we interact with people who are different from us.

If you choose to engage in an active Guided Accountability pairing, you are committing to meet with this partner once a week for 45 minutes. You will need to find a consistent time to meet, and you must be able to uphold the commitment to that time. Partnerships fall apart when these meetings are not honored. We are creating a culture of accountability, and we must all take responsibility for our parts in the equation.

— — — — — — — — — — — —

You might find yourself saying, "I'm not quite ready to be in a Guided Accountability pairing," to which I say: "No Problem."

— — — — — — — — — — — —

I appreciate how seriously you're taking this commitment. I encourage you to take up an active listening role in the community. As you feel comfortable, let your voice be heard. You'll be surprised by how much support you receive. Remember, this is *not* about the A-roll life. This isn't the 'reel' from social media feeds. This is the truth. The dirty, nitty-gritty stuff we crop out of photos. It's REAL. It's oftentimes the best part of who we are, and we are going to leverage this truth-telling to create an unstoppable force the likes of which this world has never seen.

So, when you're ready, grab yourself a partner and hit the road running. If more than a month goes by, and you're still a little gun shy, reach out to the community. We'd love to talk you through any limiting beliefs that may be holding you back, and help you better assess your situation.

WHAT IF I FAIL? You've already won JUST by reading this far. You've already won by showing up. You cannot fail. Success is in showing up for your partner and yourself week after week. That's it.

I DON'T THINK I CAN DO THIS. If you can dedicate one hour per week of focused time where you channel your energy into your partner and your goals, you *can* do this. Statistically, the one hour you dedicate to your partner has a five-times return. The clarity you achieve when carving out your space makes you a more effective decision-maker and a far more effective action-taker. Remember: Just keep taking the next right step.

I'M READY TO COMMIT. I'M ALL IN! . . . NOW WHAT?

First, brace yourself for the most life-changing experience you can imagine.

The rest is pretty simple: Just leap. We've already built the net to catch you.

Thank you for giving us the honor and privilege of accompanying you on this journey to your best, most inspired self.

ABOUT THE AUTHOR

C harlena Smith is living proof that every single one of us has the ability to overcome adversity time and time again and create the most extraordinary life we can imagine.

When Charlena was in her early 20s, she "had it all" by nearly every definition. She was the first in her family to go *away* to college, and she went on to earn four undergraduate and three graduate degrees, as well as a traditional MBA. She was a full-time college professor and researcher of human communication at Towson University and the COO of 83North,

a thriving and rapidly expanding full-service marketing company on the East Coast. She was married to a brilliant NASA
rocket scientist, and they lived in a beautiful rural home:
white picket fence, dog, and all.

When Charlena and her husband Scott decided to add
a baby to their family, things got a little complicated. Two
back-to-back pregnancies were really hard on Charlena. She
had hyperemesis gravidarum (HG) during both pregnancies
which, in layman's terms, is consistent, constant, ever-present
vomiting. She was hospitalized a great deal of the time to
keep both her and the babies safe. She was fed intravenously
through total parenteral nutrition lines that went straight to
her heart, because she was starving to death. After the birth
of her first son, Keegan, the HG lifted at 6 weeks postpartum.
When she had her second, Colby, it never lifted. She pursued
specialist after specialist for answers, to no avail.

Meanwhile, taking care of two babies under two is HARD
WORK. Without a non-bias partner to serve as a mirror,
Charlena actually found herself in a complex kind of denial
about her medical condition and found that working – re-
lentlessly – was easier than staying home. So she kept at her
role as full-time professor, and as COO, and added to the list
"PhD candidate." She continued to pursue answers for what
was going on inside her body and had nearly starved to death
at 97 pounds when she finally had a breakthrough moment.
She vomited bile right in front of a surgeon in his office. The

response? "We're going to perform an exploratory surgery tomorrow morning. What just happened isn't physically possible. This is NOT all in your head." And so, the long and winding road to healing, by nearly dying, began.

At 30 years of age, with two children under two, Charlena and her family were told there was no chance of survival. 0%. Major medical institutions like Johns Hopkins and University of Maryland turned her away, claiming they weren't hospice care, and that's all it would be. When her heart continued to beat long after her projected expiration date, despite Acute Respiratory Distress Syndrome, multiple collapsed lungs, and an open wound in her abdomen from her chest to her hip bone, she was told she would never be able to sit up on her own again, let alone stand or walk. She would never be able to eat or speak and would be on a ventilator for the rest of her life.

Defying the logic of doctors and the temptation of taking on a victim mentality, she has gone on, through years of rehab, to not only walk and talk, but RUN, leap, and play with her husband and two beautiful children, travel the world for pleasure and as an international speaker, and successfully jumpstart a nonprofit marketing company aptly named The Girl Who Lived.

As a professor, on the first day of class each semester, Charlena would share the analogy of a "full" life in terms of the empty or full jar to her grad students. If you haven't heard it, here's a summary of what would happen in her classrooms. Charlena would stand at the front of the room with a mason jar and then fill it with two-inch rocks. She'd ask the class if the jar was full? Yes, they'd agree. Then she would pour a box of pebbles into the jar, and they would roll into the open areas between the rocks. Again, she'd ask if the jar was full. The students would chuckle and agree that, yes, this time it was full. But Charlena would then begin to let loose a handful of sand into the jar. The sand would trickle in and filled the space between the pebbles. Full? Timid this time, the class would more ask than answer, "Yes?" Then she'd pour from her own water bottle to "truly" fill up the jar. The point being that if they wanted a truly full and complete life, they should put the big rocks in first!

Charlena's greatest gift had been this very analogy she'd heard from another professor and continued to share with her own students year after year. Her jar had been *completely* 100% emptied for her. There were no rocks. There were no pebbles. No sand or water. She was in the ICU on life support, being read her final rights. Her jar was empty. She had to make a decision. She CHOSE to put "herself" back in that jar first. She worked *hard* to do it. First, at not dying. Then, at the basic steps of living: learning to breathe, sit, stand, walk, talk, drink, and eat again. Then, she got to CHOOSE what to put back in her jar. At what speed and in what order. From that moment on, Charlena's life has been incredibly intentional. And the result of living a life that is in alignment with her purpose and her values...well, let's just say she'd call it priceless. And there, in the filling of her own jar, were the beginnings of Guided Accountability. She developed and used the process to transform her reality and define a new possibility for her future.

The next piece of the puzzle came through her work with The Girl Who Lived (TGWL). Charlena set up communication structures for one of her clients, the International Rescue Committee (IRC). TGWL was tasked with setting up a system to acclimate Syrians into the U.S. culture as smoothly as possible. They needed to learn to navigate not only a new landscape and different language, but also different medical, transportation, and school systems, just to name a few. TGWL developed a system that paired each refugee with an established woman in the community nearby and created a communication framework to help them navigate the language and cultural barriers. The framework was wildly successful. Not only were the Syrians acclimating faster than ever, but their American counterparts flooded TGWL and the IRC with comments, testifying to their changed hearts and the ability to access empathy in a way they'd never dreamed possible. It was life-changing in the best way for both parties.

And then it clicked: "Wait. Is this a thing? If we pair women and use this kind of framework – give them space, time, and permission to be vulnerable, along with the tools to discover their purpose and live it out – will we get the same results?"

Charlena decided to find out, so she began a beta test with other women around the world. That's how Optio and the Guided Accountability movement were born.

Charlena compiled loads of research and catalogued an intense amount of data from her pairings. A top NASA engineer (who just so happens to be that amazing partner who was mentioned earlier...) created a complex algorithm to pair people to their best Guided Accountability partners. The research proved that the best partner for you in a Guided pairing is not a best friend, but rather the person who is going to bring OUT the best in you. Charlena continued, armed with an algorithm, to create deep, thoughtful trainings on how to be a Guided Accountability partner, plus a specific framework for women to discover their true purpose, develop goals in alignment with that purpose, and see it through in a 12-week program that results in a 97% increase in success rates. Every time.

Charlena continues to run Optio, work alongside refugees, and play every single day with her family.

Charlena is also a top-rated international keynote speaker. While corporations, associations, and nonprofits regularly bring Charlena in to speak at their conferences and workshops, she has a special passion for positively impacting women. Charlena strongly believes that in order to truly change the world, we MUST empower our women first.

To contact Charlena about media appearances, coaching, speaking at your event, or to subscribe to her mailing list to stay on top of her − and her family's − always entertaining adventures, visit www.charlenasmith.com

BOOK CHARLENA TO SPEAK

Best-selling Author
Charlena Smith

BOOK CHARLENA TO SPEAK

Booking Charlena as your Keynote Speaker guarantees a highly enjoyable and unforgettable event!

For two decades, Charlena has been a top-rated professor by her students and fellow professors. Her passion for teaching and learning make for a dynamic educational environment enjoyed by one and all.

Charlena loves bringing Guided Accountability into corporations through her work with Optio (www.myoptio.org). Please reach out if you would be interested in increasing the successful completion of your corporate goals by 97%. Charlena thrives on team-building exercises and has a long-standing track record of corporate success.

For more than a decade, Charlena Smith has also been consistently rated as a top international Keynote Speaker by meeting planners *and* attendees. Her unique style combines inspiring audiences with her unbelievable TRUE stories, keeping them laughing until they cry with her positive energy and stand-up comedy style delivery, and empowering them with actionable strategies to take all they've learned to the next level. Every human that walks away from an event where Charlena speaks leaves feeling inspired. Empowered. Like they can conquer the world. THAT is Charlena's superpower as a speaker.

For more information, visit www.CharlenaSmith.com

RESOURCES AND RECOMMENDATIONS FOR FURTHER READING

'm a big believer in continual personal development. We should always be training to be the best version of ourselves. I'm a voracious reader and attend as many seminars and conferences as I can without disrupting the flow of my family (I frequently bring them with me – BIG shout out to seminars that include kids!). One of the guiding principles of Guided Accountability is to see through windows that would typically remain unseen and un-experienced. I love to challenge my own thinking, my own view of the world, and re-imagine what's possible on a regular basis. If you, too, are of this mindset, you'll love some of these books below.

— — — — — — — — — — —

The Miracle Morning: The Not-So-Obvious Secret Guaranteed to Transform Your Life (Before 8am) by Hal Elrod

Why We Do What We Do: Understanding Self-Motivation by Edward Deci with Richard Flaste

Everything is Figureoutable by Marie Forleo

The Surprising Truth About What Motivates Us by Daniel Pink

168 Hours: You Have More Time Than You Think by Laura Vanderkam

The Four Agreements by Don Miguel Ruiz

Emotional Intelligence 2.0 by Travis Bradberry and Jean Greaves

Get a PhD in You by Julie Reisler

Front Row Factor by Jon Vroman

Atomic Habits: Tiny Changes, Remarkable Results: An Easy & Proven Way to Build Good Habits & Break Bad Ones by James Clear

Better Than Before by Gretchen Rubin

The Road Back to You: An Enneagram Journey to Self-Discovery by Ian Morgan Cron and Suzanne Stabile

Boss Mom by Dana Malstaff

The Gifts of Imperfection by Brené Brown

Dare to Lead by Brené Brown

OTHER AWESOME TOOLS

Meditation and mindfulness don't come naturally to me. I have to work hard at it. Two apps that have helped me a great deal in this space are Headspace and Insight Timer.

ThinkUp is a fantastic app for creating your personalized affirmations that we walk through in Guided Accountability.

LET'S CONNECT

I love meeting like-minded people with a growth mindset and sharing all the amazing resources floating around out there! It is also really amazing to hear from people who have been impacted in some way by reading one of my books or hearing me speak on stage, on podcasts, or in videos. I would absolutely love to know what you're implementing in your own life (that would REALLY fill my bucket!) or answer any questions you might have. I truly enjoy a good dialogue and love to make my systems and processes better and remain fully connected. Please feel free to reach out via Instagram – @Charlena_Shrieves – or Facebook – @Charlena.Shrieves – and click on the connect/message tab (Yes – they're both from my maiden name – and I want to keep you on the inside, friend. So I've shown you how to get into the inside circle, just like that!). I look forward to connecting with you and promise to offer any value I can bring.

A QUICK FAVOR

If the concept of Guided Accountability has helped you in any way, please share. The only way we'll have a positive impact on our communities, and the world, is by sharing this systematic approach to deep connection. Don't keep it to yourself. We'll only shake the ground if we do it together. I am incredibly grateful for the life experiences I had at such young ages that brought me to the realization and concepts outlined in this book, but I would much rather the world be able to learn these lessons in a quick read than by nearly dying. Just think: whose life could you impact if you share?

Here are a few ways to help spread the word:

- Write a review on Amazon (seriously, guys…you have no idea how big of a deal this is. It's HUGE).
- Share your copy of this book with a friend. Physically hand them your printed copy, or lend them the electronic copy. We intentionally calibrated the settings to allow sharing because we want everyone to be able to experience Guided Accountability and the amazing success it results in.
- Buy a copy for a friend! It makes a great gift. Especially if you find a Guided Accountability partner – you can both work through it at the same time!

SO MANY WAYS TO STAY CONNECTED

www.CharlenaSmith.com

www.facebook.com/guidedaccountability
www.instagram.com/guidedaccountability

www.facebook.com/charlena.shrieves
www.instagram.com/charlena_shrieves

www.facebook.com/myoptio
www.instagram.com/myoptio_org
www.myoptio.org

Charlena@myoptio.org

APPENDIX

The following pages, referenced throughout *Guided Accountability*, are taken directly from Optio's Planner. You can use these pages to inspire your own Guided Accountability planner, or order one directly through Amazon or where most books are sold.

**Picture where you will be 60 days from now. See it. Smell it. Feel it. Breathe it in.
In order to get there you must achieve a few big milestones along the way. Place
those milestones on your 60 day path.** These milestones are not things you need to
overcome, they're life unfolding FOR you – to get you where you need to go. Close your
eyes and picture these milestones. Imagine yourself triumphant, overcoming obstacles as
if they were just pebbles along your path. Use this outlook to prepare for life, the expected
and the unexpected. **Remember: you were born to do this**. Any obstacles are
just part of your overall story of awesomeness.

MAJOR GOALS

PRIORITIES

1

2

3

4

5

6

Months: _____ *to* _____

MON	TUES	WED	THURS	FRI	SAT/SUN

MON	TUES	WED	THURS	FRI	SAT/SUN

Six weeks from now you will thank yourself for starting today.

Partner: _____

> **Optio Pledge as a Guide:**
> *I pledge to hold you accountable with integrity.*

KNOW YOU:

With regard to your chosen section of the life wheel, what do you say to yourself, about yourself, when you are alone?

SEE YOU:

What do you want to say to yourself, about yourself?

FACE YOU:

What most prevents you from being who you want to be? This may be what you tell yourself through self-limiting beliefs, past experiences, poor planning, financial limitations, lack of vision, role models or examples, time limitations, lack of focus, or skills needed. How will you flip these obstacles to become ladders, lifting you to your goals? Focus on what you can control.

BELIEVE YOU:

Sculpt an affirmation that reflects who you will be this season with regard to your life wheel selection. Use powerful, uplifting words that inspire you to believe in YOU, and know that YOU can crush your goals.

AFFIRMATION *(Write your partner's affirmation here)*

Have your partner repeat her affirmation three times. Mirror it back to her with conviction.

KNOW IT: *What 60 day goal can your partner focus on this season that will actively transform her into her affirmation? Be sure to dig into her 'why' – what is her real motivation?*

_____

_____

SEE IT: *Encourage your partner to visualize herself achieving her goal and truly becoming her affirmation. What does it look like? Feel like? Smell like? Now visualize the obstacles that will arise: Develop a plan for how she will overcome them.*

FACE IT: *Encourage your partner to name any fears that may arise. Acknowledge their presence, and let them go.*

BELIEVE IT: *Encourage your partner to see her own potential.*

COMMITMENT THIS WEEK: *Encourage your partner to make a commitment to take two active and specific steps this week toward crushing their 60 day goal, and becoming her affirmation (you will repeat this action every week):*

- _____
- _____

Boldly state your affirmation again and have your Optio mirror it back to you.

Date: _____

"

Optio Pledge as Guided:
I pledge to offer my authentic self.

"

KNOW YOU:
....

"Women need real moments of solitude and self-reflection to balance out how much of ourselves we give away" - *Barbara De Angelis.*

SEE YOU:
....

"With realization of one's own potential and self-confidence in one's ability, one can build a better world" - *Dalai Lama.*

FACE YOU:
....

"We cannot solve our problems with the same thinking we used when we created them" - *Albert Einstein*

BELIEVE YOU:
....

"When you catch a glimpse of your potential, that's when passion is born" - *Zig Ziglar*

AFFIRMATION *(Write your affirmation here)*

KNOW IT: *What 60 day goal are you focusing on crushing this season that actively transforms you into your affirmation? Why is this goal important to you?*

_____

_____

SEE IT: *Visualize yourself crushing your goal and becoming your affirmation. What will it look like when you do? Visualize obstacles and how you will overcome them.*

FACE IT: *Verbalize any fears or doubts that arise.*

BELIEVE IT: *Leap, and the net will appear." - John Burroughs*

COMMITMENT THIS WEEK: *Remember, all progress takes place outside the comfort zone: Be bold. Make a commitment to your partner that you will take two active and specific steps this week toward crushing your 60 day goal, and becoming your affirmation. Write them here:*

⬤ _____

⬤ _____

Boldly state your affirmation again and have your Optio mirror it back to you.   7

Theme: _____

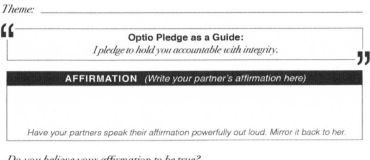

Optio Pledge as a Guide:
I pledge to hold you accountable with integrity.

AFFIRMATION *(Write your partner's affirmation here)*

Have your partners speak their affirmation powerfully out loud. Mirror it back to her.

Do you believe your affirmation to be true?

YES

How did her affirmation empower and uplift her this week? If it came easily: encourage your partner to challenge herself further. Stretch her outside of her comfort zone.

NO

If they're not convinced: Why? What can be handled differently this week to expand the limiting beliefs they've placed on themselves and their circumstances?

LOOKING BACK

Did you accomplish the goals you set last week?

YES

What did she accomplish?
How did it make her feel with regard to her affirmation?

NO

What intentions were left unfulfilled?
What prevented her from achieving her goal?

LOOKING FORWARD

Encourage your partner to visualize herself accomplishing her goal. Visualize the path it will take to get there. See the potential obstacles that she may encounter. Visualize how she will overcome those obstacles. Be realistic, but bold: What two steps can she take this week? How can she apply this week's theme to her goals?

Remember: We are always 'in progress'. Her goals may be the same. As she grows her goals may shift. Progress is a wonderful thing, but remind her to always remain accountable.

How can your partner apply this week's theme to their specific goals? How can you see her using this week's theme to grow as an individual and an accountability partner?

Boldly state your affirmation again and have your Optio mirror it back to you.

WEEKLY WISDOM

Partner: _____ *Date:* _____

Optio Pledge as Guided:
I pledge to offer my authentic self.

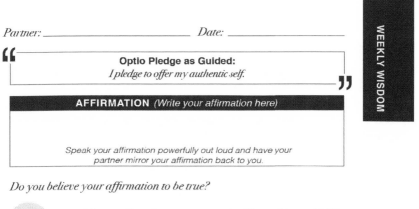

AFFIRMATION *(Write your affirmation here)*

*Speak your affirmation powerfully out loud and have your
partner mirror your affirmation back to you.*

Do you believe your affirmation to be true?

YES   How did your affirmation empower and uplift you this week? If it came easily: how can you challenge yourself further?

....

NO   If you're not convinced: Why? What can be handled differently this week to expand the limiting beliefs you've placed on yourself and your circumstances?

LOOKING BACK

Did you accomplish the goals you set with your partner last week?

YES   What did you accomplish?
How did it make you feel with regard to your affirmation?

....

NO   What intentions were left unfulfilled?
What prevented you from achieving your goal?

LOOKING FORWARD

Visualize yourself accomplishing your goal. Visualize the path it will take to get there. See the potential obstacles that you may encounter. Visualize how you will overcome those obstacles. Be realistic, but bold: What two steps will you take this week? How will you apply this week's theme to your goals?

Remember: We are always 'in progress'. Your goals may be the same. As you grow your goals may shift. Progress is a wonderful thing, but always remain accountable.

How can you apply this week's theme to your specific goals? How can you use this week's theme to grow as an individual and an accountability partner?

Boldly state your affirmation again and have your Optio mirror it back to you.

*Week:*_____

BIG WINS:

- _____ - _____
- _____ - _____
- _____ - _____
- _____ - _____

REVIEW YOUR GOAL AND ASSESS YOUR PROGRESS

How did you spend your time this week?

- _____
- _____
- _____

How will you improve next week?

- _____
- _____
- _____

NEXT WEEK'S FOCUS

HABITS YOU'RE FOCUSING ON DEVELOPING

LOOKING FORWARD PLAN

What is the one thing you can do each day next week that will make everything else easier?

MON	TUES	WED

CHALLENGE YOURSELF
to learn something new

BUDGET

$ IN: ....

$ OUT: ....

Live the length AND width of your life.

REWRITE YOUR 60 DAY GOAL ....

REWRITE YOUR WEEKLY GOAL ....

Write the actions you will take to meet these goals:

- _____
- _____
- _____
- _____

BIGGEST LESSON LEARNED ....

THURS	FRI	SAT	SUN

Today is: _____   M T W Th F Sa Su

┌─ **AFFIRMATION** *(Write your affirmation here)* ─────────────────┐
│   │
│   │
│   │
│   │
└───┘

MORNING REVIEW

This morning I am grateful for: *What will make today a win:*

○ _____   ○ _____
○ _____   ○ _____
○ _____   ○ _____
○ _____   ○ _____
○ _____   ○ _____

TODAY'S PRIORITIES

1
2
3
4

FOCUS *(your one thing)*

EXERCISE/MEAL PLAN

PERSONAL GROWTH

BUDGET *(where's your money going?)*

HOURLY SCHEDULE

6am _____

7am _____

8am _____

9am _____

10am _____

11am _____

12pm _____

1pm _____

2pm _____

3pm _____

4pm _____

5pm _____

6pm _____

7pm _____

8pm _____

9pm _____

10pm _____

TO DO TODAY:

DAILY GOALS

Do something today that your future self will thank you for.

END-OF-DAY REVIEW

Tonight I am grateful for:

_____

_____

_____

_____

Today's wins (Brag Girl! Brag!):

_____

_____

_____

_____

How I'll improve tomorrow:

_____

_____

_____

35

Partner: _____

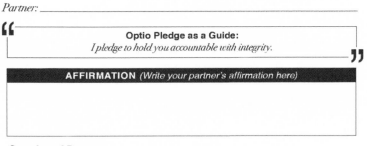

Optio Pledge as a Guide:
I pledge to hold you accountable with integrity.

AFFIRMATION *(Write your partner's affirmation here)*

Overview of Progress:

Have your partner look back at her micro goals in sum. How far has she gone toward her macro goal? Does she feel accomplished? Point out to her the various areas YOU have seen personal growth in HER? Does she feel like she has truly brought her affirmation to life? Has she lived it out? What has the impact been?

Rollover Goals:

If your partner has unfulfilled intentions from this season - ask her if she wants to roll them over into next season. Or, ask her if she's reevaluated her priorities, and they're no longer at the top? If she wants to roll them over - encourage her to make note of them for her next accountability partner.

Was it still a successful season? Did you grow? Did you learn from your failures? How can you apply what you learned to create future success?

_____

_____

Keepsakes for Next Season:

Encourage your partner to look back at the season: Are there any 'best practices' that she'd like to take with her moving forward? Did she discover anything about herself that she doesn't want to forget? Ask her about your effectiveness at holding her accountable: What did you do well? What could you improve upon for your next partner? What worked? What didn't? How have the Weekly Wisdom themes applied throughout your season?

_____

_____

ACKNOWLEDGMENTS

Acknowledge your Optio partner for bringing her authentic self this season. It takes strength to show vulnerability to strangers. Acknowledge her for the unique gifts she brought to the partnership: use specific examples from your time together. Acknowledgments should generate a feeling of love and appreciation for one another, and bring a sense of completion to the season.

Boldly state your affirmation again and have your Optio mirror it back to you.

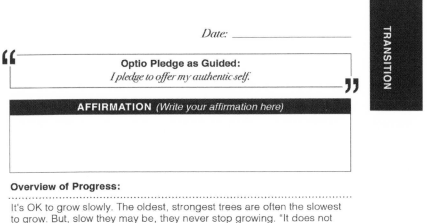

Date: _____

> ## Optio Pledge as Guided:
> *I pledge to offer my authentic self.*

AFFIRMATION *(Write your affirmation here)*

Overview of Progress:

It's OK to grow slowly. The oldest, strongest trees are often the slowest to grow. But, slow they may be, they never stop growing. "It does not matter how slowly you go as long as you do not stop" - *Confucius*

Rollover Goals:

"A goal is not always meant to be reached, it often serves simply as something to aim at." - *Bruce Lee*

Was it still a successful season? Did you grow? Did you learn from your failures? How can you apply what you learned to create future success?

_____

_____

Keepsakes for Next Season:

Encourage your partner to look back at the season: Are there any 'best practices' that you'd like to take with you moving forward? Did you discover anything about yourself that you don't want to forget? Think about your partner's effectiveness at holding you accountable: What worked? What didn't? How have the Weekly Wisdom themes applied throughout your season?

_____

_____

ACKNOWLEDGMENTS

Acknowledge your Optio partner for holding you accountable this season. Acknowledge her for the unique gifts she brought to the partnership: use specific examples from your time together. Acknowledgments should generate a feeling of love and appreciation for one another, and bring a sense of completion to the season.

Boldly state your affirmation again and have your Optio mirror it back to you.

62316089R00073

Made in the USA
Middletown, DE
23 August 2019